THE DEFINITIVE GUIDE TO TWITTER MARKETING

(I double-dog dare you to try it!)

Bridget Willard

BridgetWillard.com

Copyright © 2021 Bridget Willard

All rights reserved

The characters and events portrayed in this book are fictitious. Any similarity to real persons, living or dead, is coincidental and not intended by the author.

No part of this book may be reproduced, or stored in a retrieval system, or transmitted in any form or by any means, electronic, mechanical, photocopying, recording, or otherwise, without express written permission of the publisher.

ISBN-13: 9798590696833
ISBN-10: 1477123456

Cover design by: Art Painter
Library of Congress Control Number: 2018675309
Printed in the United States of America

CONTENTS

Title Page
Copyright
Foreword
Preface
The Definitive Guide to Twitter Marketing   1
Introduction   2
Optimize Your Bio   5
Be Present   8
Follow Everyone   10
Make Lists   13
Don't Use Too Many Hashtags   15
Format Your Tweets   17
Use Short Links   20
Share Other People's Content   22
Read Articles Before You Share Them   24
The Reply Button is Powerful   26

Participate in Twitter Chats	30
Share Your Blog Posts	35
Let People Know You're Accepting Clients	37
Be a Polite Human	40
Reply to Every Tweet	42
Don't Forget Where You Came From	43
Share YouTube Videos	45
Use Twitter for Business Development	48
Give People Credit	50
Use the Native App	54
Be Consistent	56
Follow People in Your Industry	58
Follow People in Your City	60
Spend 5 Minutes a Day in your Home Feed	62
Log in with Intent	65
Look at Your Analytics	67
Cycle Your Content	69
Don't Use the Retweet Button	74
Be Patient	76
Twitter Marketing is a Long Game!	78
Bibliography	79
About The Author	85

FOREWORD

It's not a coincidence that Bridget asked me to write the foreword to this book -- I met Bridget via a Twitter post about WordCamp Europe in Berlin. We were still traveling the globe and meeting in large groups in close proximity then. Today we spend much of our social time on some sort of media, whether it be Zoom, Facebook, Twitter, or TikTok.

Be polite, patient, share, be present -- the secrets of Twitter success sound much the same as how we can be successful in any relationship -- and let's be quite clear, social media is a relationship, and it's long term. I have spent the last year building up my own Twitter platform, emulating Bridget step-by-step. I'm really happy with how many followers I have, but I'm even happier with what I've achieved and the time I've had with Bridget learning from each other.

Social empathy is a constant topic in the many

classes I teach in Online Marketing. It's an important part of what makes us happy and conscious members of a healthy society. It's an integral part of what makes our business a success.

When I first began in marketing, we were going door to door with gift certificates for a free cocktail at the seafood restaurant where I was employed. Face-to-face was augmented by fax marketing and fun radio commercials. Today we often never see the face of our visitors and customers, but the rules haven't really changed that much. Find out what people want, give it to them at a fair price, and make sure they return with a friend.

#ThinkLikeBridget. I saw this on Twitter somewhere, and it wasn't in a post from Bridget, but one of her clients. We're lucky when people sing our praises, and lift us up above the crowd. The internet is a busy place. Raise yourself, your business, and your clients up above the crowd. As you will discover in this book, Twitter success is a long game and requires patience. But hey - if you give up, you can't succeed.

~ Warren Laine-Naida
Marketing Consultant, Teacher, SEO Guru, Author, Chef, and Friend

warrenlainenaida.net

PREFACE

This marketplace is full of fluff marketing books that promise success in three easy steps. Or they are full of platitudes that make you feel excited to start but have no actionable content. I'm pretty famous (or infamous) for advice that actually works. That's my NO B.S. Promise.

There is no easy way to gain 10,000 followers. You can do it if you are willing to put in the work and spend the time.

If you're willing to read this book (which will take less than an hour), and implement the tactics for a month, my bet is that you will see the results you've been looking for.

I double-dog dare you.

"She'll tell you what she thinks is best regardless if it is what you think you want to hear, she'll challenge you to think broadly about your vision and goals with social, and she'll curate storytelling into each component of your content strategy." Michelle Keefer

"Bridget's Twitter coaching has been transformational." Joceyln Mozak

"I look to Bridget for advice on how to make my own improvements. I trust her knowledge and she spends a lot of time researching and implementing what she learns in Social Media. Bridget is always open to answer my questions, which you don't find very often. I'd say she's a true leader!" Amy Donohue

"Her awesome Twitter tips, tricks and thought-provoking discussions make her one of my favourite marketers to follow." Allison Smith

"She is an excellent trainer and communicator, and did a fine job of never making anyone feel overwhelmed." Katie Rexrode

"Bridget is someone I look up to for Social Media expertise on a daily basis. As someone who was new to Twitter, I relied on Bridget's examples of how to successfully engage and grow an audience." Kendra Hubbard

THE DEFINITIVE GUIDE TO TWITTER MARKETING

By Bridget Willard

INTRODUCTION

✽ ✽ ✽

Twitter marketing is valuable, yet so many businesses undervalue Twitter in their overall marketing strategy. It's super sad. Let's fix that. I know you can improve with a few tweaks.

After implementing all of this advice and about six months of practice, you'll be as good as I am. Awesome. You can rock your company's marketing world or go start a social media management agency. Why not?

And, if you're ever curious, go look at my Twitter account[1]. Unlike most "marketing experts on Twitter," **I model the behavior I preach.** Also, since I've written about Twitter extensively since 2011, I'll be quoting myself -- a lot.

If you're looking for a refresher on Twitter[2], I suggest that you start with my 10-series videos on YouTube.

   https://bit.ly/LearnTwitter2020

Each video is less than 10 minutes long. **Please don't skip a video because you think you know it**. I give insight beyond the beginner lesson in each video that builds throughout the course. It's free and shorter than a movie.

Here is the Ultimate Guide to Twitter Marketing in 2021

OPTIMIZE YOUR BIO

❈ ❈ ❈

The first thing you'll want to do when you start your Twitter account, or get serious about marketing with Twitter, is optimize your bio. Your bio is your elevator pitch and your first opportunity to get people interested.

Think about flirting in dating. You want people to be interested but still understand what you're all about. "I provide solutions for your clients" is too vague. Every business provides solutions for their clients. What kind of solutions do you offer? Do you build websites? Say that. Are you a gift shop owner? Say that. Do you write novels? Say that.

- Pin a tweet to your profile that leads to your website! This is super important.

Twitter shows your bio in the sidebar on related tweets, when people hover over your username, and in emails from Twitter. This is important real estate. Don't clog it up with hashtags or emoji (that goes for your name, too). Make this easy to scan.

Using generic keywords in your bio, meaning writing for your customer, is how Twitter will suggest your profile to other people. I literally got a new client in December of 2020 because my account was suggested to them. So, yes, you can get work from Twitter.

> "Your account should have a header, a clear photo, a website, and a bio. Your bio should be clear to people outside of your niche and be optimized for keywords."
> Bridget Willard (Willard)

Make sure your logo fits in the circle of a 500 x 500-pixel square. It should be clear on a mobile phone. Test it. Don't trust your 42" monitor. That's not how most people see your brand. Your Twitter header should also be clear.

If you use a photo for your avatar, make sure your face is clear. It shouldn't be shaded by a hat or be covered with a face mask. The point of a photo as your profile picture is to create a connection with the user. This also helps you stand out in the home feed while people are scrolling.

Remember, people go to your Twitter profile once. They want to see who you are and whether or not you're interesting enough to follow. Or they may have been referred to your business and they're validating the information they have. Is your online presence consistent? They use all of these signals to decide if they want to work with you.

> "People aren't going to your Instagram bio, your Facebook page, your Twitter profile if they already know you." Bridget Willard (WPwatercooler Network)

BE PRESENT

❋ ❋ ❋

One of the best tips to marketing yourself or your brand on Twitter is to be present. Make it a point to sign in with purpose or intent. No one likes talking to a distracted person at a party. It's the same on Twitter.

Pay attention to your notifications and be in that conversation. Yes, it could take hours for a reply, and it is totally fine to respond later. With that said, how would you like to be treated online?

If you say hello to someone in person and they don't respond or acknowledge you, how do you feel? Would you like to be ignored? Most people don't.

Being present also means being self-aware. Be at your best online. Remember when you'd go to someone else's house when you were a kid and your mom told you to be on your best behavior? Do that online.

It is way too easy to tweet off a quick response or a flippant answer or a stream of consciousness that isn't edited and lacks sensitivity. How do I know? I've done it. I'm not proud of those moments, but we all have them. A few of my friends have texted me after those moments saying, "Are you okay?"

As much as you can, be present on Twitter. Are you angry, annoyed, upset? Get off the internet. Go for a walk. Calm down. It's not that you shouldn't be upset, but you should never react online; always respond. That's how to be present on Twitter.

> "It's tempting to react to political news from your brand on Twitter. Unless your brand is Saturday Night Live, don't do it. You'll be fueling trolls and undermining your brand. It's your brand. Protect it." Bridget Willard (Willard)

FOLLOW EVERYONE

❋ ❋ ❋

It's funny how many people use social media in a backward way. They use media for their own opinions, marketing, and entourage building. That's just an RSS feed or Press Releases. If that's what you want to do, so be it. Don't expect Twitter marketing to "work" for you.

Marketing is a social science. Twitter Marketing is about people and what they do and what they like and how they respond. The only way you can understand the gorillas is to go be with them. Watch. Listen. Observe. Then you'll know how to get closer to the silverback as Dian Fossey[3] did.

The first thing your brand communicates on Twitter when your following to followers ratio is lopsided is that you don't care about anyone else. So, why should they follow you? The person who stumbles upon your account with 50,000 followers who only has 96 knows you don't care.

They may follow you because now you look like a celebrity and, for some reason, we give celebrities a pass. Or you may only be listed. Either way, it is a great way to be off-putting to your audience, show that you are tone-deaf, and more.

Okay, if you're Nike or Chevrolet or Apple, you can do that. However, most of my readers are small business owners. You're excited to get your first 1,000 followers on Twitter. By the way, the first thousand is the hardest. The only way you will get those is by following people back.

> "To get customers on Twitter it is important that you are — are you ready for this? — social. People always think of the media part of "social media" and conveniently forget the work part. Yes. The work is to interact with others." Bridget Willard

As an aside, Twitter has following to follower glass ceilings at 1:1. If you're following 2,000 people but only 200 people are following you, then you won't be able to follow any more people until that ratio is closer to 2,000:2,000. This is a quirk of Twitter as no other social media platform does this.

I've experienced these limits at 2,000, 5,000, 9,000, 14,000, and 19,000 followers. The largest account I ever grew was Riggins Construction[4] at 20,000 which took six years from 2009-2015 before I left to start my marketing career.

This is why I unfollow people who don't follow me back. I use who.unfollowed.me for this.

MAKE LISTS

❄ ❄ ❄

Creating lists on Twitter is vital to your Twitter marketing. This allows you to segregate your followers by demographic giving you the power of a focus group at the click of your mouse.

My ultimate guide to using Twitter lists[5] is a great starting point for how to start a list and which lists you should create.

Twitter lists enable me, as a one-person shop, to personally and successfully manage so many Twitter clients. I'm not outsourcing my Twitter work. No, I do as much manually as possible. Why? Because a good suit is tailored to the person. You can get a cheaper suit at Men's Warehouse, but it won't fit as well.

Effective Twitter Marketing means that you are spending as much time interacting with humans as possible. Understand them. How are their views shifting? What do they like? What don't they like?

WordPress products and agencies often purchase swag for conferences that they think is cool. But if they spent time reading tweets from their audience, they would know what the people would think is cool -- and useful.

Don't just order a fidget spinner because it's a fad. Why? Because your product isn't a fad. It isn't a distraction. It's serious.

The best way to approach Twitter Marketing is with an ear to listen.

DON'T USE TOO MANY HASHTAGS

❖ ❖ ❖

The goal of Twitter marketing is to entice people to read your tweet and click on your link or profile. Hashtags can distract from that goal. So many people see hashtags written everywhere that they have the impression that adding a hashtag is magic. Boom. You're going viral now, baby.

Even the Noom app uses hashtags in their copy. In their app! It's painful to read. I know why they are doing it. They're trying to be friendly. But man, I wish I could get them to stop doing it.

We scan; we don't read.

People on Twitter are scrolling on mobile devices. They may be using TweetDeck or Hootsuite to browse Twitter on their desktop or second monitor. Either way, the hashtag creates a link[6] (because it is a link) and it is a distraction to your call to action.

I've been using fewer and fewer hashtags lately. It isn't affecting my impressions at all. My top tweets get quite a bit of engagement even without hashtags.

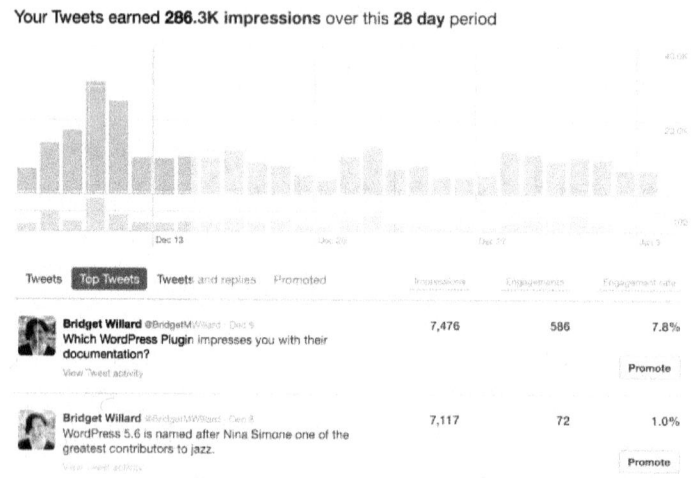

FORMAT YOUR TWEETS

❊ ❊ ❊

Knowing that your audience scans, and doesn't read, shapes how you write your Tweets.

Making your tweet scannable is a great way to be noticed. Once your tweet is noticed, people are more apt to engage with the tweet, either by replying or clicking on the link.

I presume you have your blog formatted so that Open Graph[7] will pull in your 1200 x 628 featured image and meta description.

This is how I format my tweets.

You don't have to use all 260 characters.

> [Intriguing quote or question]
>
> [Call to Action]
>
> [short link]
>
> [Hashtag1]
>
> [Hashtag2]
>
> [Hashtag3]

When it comes to emoji versus GIFs, my preference is for GIFs. First of all, they're native to Twitter. Secondly, they don't take up space or break up your body copy (which makes it hard to read).

> "GIFs go where Emoji cannot. Emoji are fantastic for decorating text messages. Emoji can be awkward when it comes to screen readers or the average user who scans messages." Bridget Willard (Willard)

Insider Tips

- Don't start a Tweet with a username. This is considered a reply. Instead, use a period first ".@bridgetmwillard thanks for the useful advice." You can also rewrite the Tweet so the username isn't first. "Wow! Thanks for the advice, @bridgetmwillard. It's very useful."
- Using GIFs in your Tweets is way more effective than emoji.
- A/B Test your tweets if you don't believe me. Hashtags aren't magic.
- Mix up how you share your blog post. Extract quotes. Don't just share the headline over and over again.
- Auto DMs are a great way to get unfollowed.

USE SHORT LINKS

※ ※ ※

I'm a huge fan of short links. Long links get cut off and are ugly. As a user, I notice that I will pass over tweets that have ugly links. They're too hard to copy/paste RT (Old School RT) and I just figure the person isn't social. They're probably automating their tweets which means they probably won't reply.

With that said, I personally use Revive Old Post[8] on my site. My blog posts are cycled every x amount of hours and I have my Bitly.com API key so that the links are shortened. You can do this, even with their free version.

When I'm curating Tweets, I like to use Google's Campaign URL Builder[9] to add my name as the referral source. I'm sneaky like that. I am, after all, the campaign. I found the tweet. Handpicked, baby. Handpicked!

Campaign URL Builder

This tool allows you to easily add campaign parameters to URLs so you can track Custom Campaigns in Google Analytics.

Enter the website URL and campaign information

Fill out the required fields (marked with *) in the form below, and once complete the full campaign URL will be generated for you. *Note: the generated URL is automatically updated as you make changes.*

* Website URL	https://presshero.co/bored-easy-web-content-to-dos/
	The full website URL (e.g. `https://www.example.com`)
* Campaign Source	bridgetwillard
	The referrer: (e.g. `google`, `newsletter`)
* Campaign Medium	twitter
	Marketing medium: (e.g. `cpc`, `banner`, `email`)

SHARE OTHER PEOPLE'S CONTENT

❈ ❈ ❈

Sharing other people's content is one of the best Twitter Marketing tactics. You came across an article in your Internet search and it gave you a wow. You learned something. You smiled. You cried. Share it.

Share it with intention. Do the work to find their Twitter handle. Don't just mindlessly press buttons. That's not hand-curation. That's random. That's pedestrian. Anyone can do that.

And while I'm at it, mindlessly using an RSS feed to automate tweets is also not the best way to do it. What if that person or business tweets about something that goes against your brand standards?

What if they love React and you have tweeted that

it's garbage? What if you're curating content for Ninja Forms and they're using Gravity Forms? It's not good versus bad. It's about alignment.

READ ARTICLES BEFORE YOU SHARE THEM

❊ ❊ ❊

Reading articles before you share them goes hand in hand with not automating your Twitter feed. This isn't always a good versus evil issue. It's about whether or not the article aligns with your brand.

Does the article require a subscription to read? This is primarily why I don't share the Financial Times anymore. I get their articles through Curio, but they don't even have four free articles a month as Harvard Business Review does. If you always share content that requires a subscription, people who follow you will start ignoring your shares.

Is the article well written? No offense to outsourcing, but it becomes obvious when a non-native speaker writes copy on a website. Even if the reader isn't fully aware of why it feels wrong, they'll bounce. That won't align with your brand.

Does the article bombard the reader with ads? This is a huge issue for me. On my phone, I can choose "reader view" in Safari. I can't choose that on my laptop. (Or maybe I just don't know how.) Either way, you get the point. It's a bad user experience.

What you share is an extension of your brand. Do you want people to associate you with that experience? I'm guessing the answer is no.

Worse, the article could advocate for something you're against. You may hate the WordPress editor but the article shows people how to use blocks in Gutenberg. You may preach about accessibility but this article doesn't even use the ARIA button role. You drive a Ford, the article is about the new Chevy truck. You get it. We call this cognitive dissonance. The audience sees it as tone-deaf and out of touch.

THE REPLY BUTTON IS POWERFUL

❋ ❋ ❋

Every time I teach Twitter Marketing, I encourage my students to use the reply button. This is the most under-utilized Twitter tool for impressions, followers, and click-throughs.

Social media is about building relationships. Twitter excels in this area. The only way to build a relationship with a person is through small talk. The chit chat that so many people dread is the back and forth on Twitter with replies.

Guess what? It works. This is how I have built every account I have. The vendors I use today, I built relationships with on Twitter. More than that 85% of my client base comes from Twitter.

Matt Moll
@MattCodeJourney

Replying to @BridgetMWillard and @WarrenLNaida

Both Accessibility and SEO :)

And if you ask me, readability too. I prefer 1000 times reading HTML that is comprehensive and the structure tells me what each thing is, rather than:

8:34 AM · Jan 3, 2021 · Twitter Web App

1 Like

Warren Laine-Naida @WarrenLNaida · 23h
Replying to @MattCodeJourney and @BridgetMWillard
Oh yes!

Bridget Willard @BridgetMWillard · Jan 3
Replying to @MattCodeJourney
That makes total sense, Matt.

Carol Stephen
@Carol_Stephen

Replying to @BridgetMWillard

Sounds perfect, B! What did you have to eat? We made salmon, garlic bread, and salad. It sounds fancy, but it all came straight from Costco.

2:38 PM · Jan 2, 2021 · Twitter Web App

1 Like

> **Bridget Willard** @BridgetMWillard · Jan 2
> Replying to @Carol_Stephen
> I had filet mignon and a salad!
>
> **Carol Stephen** @Carol_Stephen · Jan 2
> Oh, yum! What kind of wine did you have?
>
> Show replies

Noom ✓
@noom

Replying to @BridgetMWillard

😆 **To be fair, those are all pretty awesome things to have in your red category. Happy New Year's Eve, Bridget!** 🥂

7:39 PM · Dec 31, 2020 · Zendesk

1 Like

When big brands like Noom reply to my Tweets, I'm more likely to mention them again. As I have several times in this article. This is the subconscious drive to reciprocate. It's powerful. Be kind. Reply. Engage.

PARTICIPATE IN TWITTER CHATS

❊ ❊ ❊

Twitter chats are my favorite part of Twitter. This is a live chat that is threaded with a specific hashtag. They usually take place once a week at the same time and last an hour.

Sadly, this last year, I haven't made the time I should to participate in my favorite one which is #DigiBlogChat[10].

This chat is hosted by my BFF Carol Stephen and by Larry Mount. It's been going on for quite a few years[11] and is always fun and inspiring.

> "Since we crowdsource the topics for our chats, we have an extremely engaged audience. There's Tripp Braden, Randy Clark, and the enthusiastic Beth Staub. John Lewis, who also runs #Innochat is a regular. Finola, Maricar, and Mitch Mitchell regularly weigh in. My friend @MistressPrime occasionally visits. @Charles-

McCool and @jpretorious are there, too. Then there are @nina_wag and @htindesigner. We couldn't forget our friends at @interprosepr! Sandy of @CreativeWoodVT has been a friend for a long time. Loni of @JorgensonLocker is also a regular on the chat! And @JKatzaman is always making us laugh!" Carol Stephen (Stephen)

Hands down, Twitter chats are the best place to find like-minded and active people on Twitter.

There are so many great chats, it's hard to keep track of them all. I love #TwitterSmarter, #BufferChat, and #DigiBlogChat.

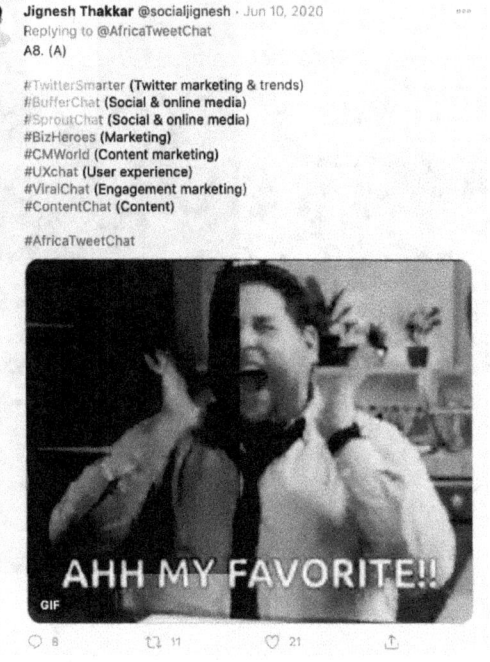

Tweet Chat Formatting

Most of the time a Twitter Chat has a specific format. The host will tweet the question with Q1, Q2, Q3, and the hashtag. Everyone else tweets with A1, A2, A3, etc with the hashtag.

Lots of people reply but that isn't necessary. Neither is quote tweeting. But if you do quote tweet, then be sure to use the hashtag in your part of the quote tweet. See why I don't like quote tweeting for Twitter chats? (Say that five times fast.)

Jim Katzaman - Get Debt-Free One Family at a Time
@JKatzaman

A1 I didn't make any health resolutions, but I'm still determined to meet my annual popcorn quota.
#DigiBlogChat

3:12 PM · Dec 29, 2020 · Twitter Web App

3 Retweets **8** Likes

Hosting a Twitter Chat

I've hosted Twitter chats in the past. They're a lot of work but great for the brand. This was primarily how I built up the Riggins Construction Twitter Account with #ConstChat[12].

It's a big-time commitment but also gives you quite a lot of content to post on your blog for your brand. I did it for a while for GiveWP but they decided not to keep it going. I posted the recap on my own blog for an example. Here's one of my recaps for SEO for Nonprofits[13]. Embedding tweets in your blog is a great way to give them a longer lifespan.

SHARE YOUR BLOG POSTS

※ ※ ※

Sharing your blog posts should be a pillar of any Twitter Marketing plan. I mean, we're all for relationships and learning but we all have to earn a living. Yes. I said it. Marketing always has a goal. You want to share your expertise online. Why not share it on Twitter?

> "People use Twitter to read and to discover information. Customers will use it to validate you the same way people use Yelp or TripAdvisor." Bridget Willard ("Your Business Marketing Should Include Twitter")

The great thing about Twitter is that *its culture tolerates volume and repetition*. This is great for marketing. It means you can share your content on Twitter as much as every third tweet! This is unheard of on any other social media platform. For clients, this is how I share their content. For myself

Of course, Twitter doesn't replace email marketing. That's the best way to get an engaged audience reading your posts. Your campaign links will tell you the story. What does Google Analytics say?

Now, this screenshot from Google Analytics shows that my average session duration (time on site) is just over a minute. That's probably because I've not been blogging as regularly as I should. Aim for two minutes.

	Social Network	Acquisition			Behavior			
		Users ↓	New Users	Sessions	Bounce Rate	Pages / Session	Avg. Session Duration	
		334	308	442	79.64%	1.50	00:01:07	
☐ 1.	Facebook	141	136	150	92.67%	1.11	00:00:14	
☐ 2.	Twitter	131	114	166	71.69%	1.71	00:01:24	
☐ 3.	(not set)	66	50	105	80.00%	1.66	00:01:48	
☐ 4.	LinkedIn	4	4	4	50.00%	2.25	00:00:42	
☐ 5.	WordPress	3	3	3	33.33%	2.00	00:00:15	
☐ 6.	YouTube	3	1	14	50.00%	1.71	00:02:16	

LET PEOPLE KNOW YOU'RE ACCEPTING CLIENTS

✽ ✽ ✽

Twitter is a great opportunity to let others know that you're accepting work or new clients. Of course, if you're a retail establishment, Twitter is great for nurturing. For business-to-business (B2B), your business model is a bit different. You're likely not selling widgets.

People ask me all the time,

"Hey, Bridget! How do you get clients?"

Me:

"Twitter."

Them:

"Well, what do you mean?"

Me:

"I'll tweet out that I'm accepting clients and then I get DMs. I schedule a meeting and then send them an invoice and go for it."

You have to tell people that you're accepting clients. Your tribe and peers on Twitter need to know. People who refer work to you need to know. It's okay to tell people you have availability. You won't look desperate.

If you're worried about how to phrase that, DM me

and I'll help you craft a tweet.

BE A POLITE HUMAN

❊ ❊ ❊

Having good manners is Twitter Marketing 101. This is the edge that the Boomers and GenXers (like me) have over Millenials and Zoomers. We make eye contact. We wait for someone to respond. We say "please," and "thank you." It matters.

> "If you're a baby boomer, you already know a lot about how to be social. For instance, would I have to ask you twice what the "magic words" are? Would you know what elements make a good letter? Could you go on a picnic and just be at the picnic, without having to whip out an electronic device? There you go! Each one of these instances is a good reason why you, as a Boomer, is a perfect candidate for social media." Carol Stephen (Stephen)

I'm not really sure where my generation went wrong with raising their kids but it is what it is. We didn't train them to have good manners. (Oh my gosh, if you're offended, I'm sorry. But seriously. Am I not wrong?)

You use Twitter for sales and marketing. All good salespeople value people -- as a person -- even if they aren't the decision-maker. This is the key to relationship marketing.

> "You have these opportunities because people know you. And because they know that you actually care about them. And the only way it works is if you actually care about them." Bridget Willard (Resnick)

REPLY TO EVERY TWEET

※ ※ ※

Everyone matters when it comes to your Twitter Marketing. When someone replies to your tweet, then answer them. If they send you a tweet, reply. If they share your definitive guide to Twitter Marketing that actually works, then thank them.

Whatever you would do if the person were standing right in front of you (socially distanced, of course) then do that.

DON'T FORGET WHERE YOU CAME FROM

❋ ❋ ❋

Do you remember how hard it was to get those first 500 followers? The first 1,000? One way to lose touch with your audience is the lack of empathy. You were once "the little guy." You were the egg on Twitter.

> "Great leaders would never sacrifice the people to save the numbers. They would sooner sacrifice the numbers to save the people." Simon Sinek (TED.com and Sinek)

When you come to Twitter with the intent to be generous, you'll demonstrate the kind of leadership that lasts. And you know how to get followers on Twitter? It's easy. Be a leader.

> "Generosity is a key attribute of leadership. We all respond well to those who give more than they take. And when they ask for favors (retweets, links, store purchases) many of us are happy to oblige. We're your biggest fans, so why not follow back?" Bridget Willard (Willard)

A person with an open mind realizes that they have something to learn from everyone. Remember how hard it was. Don't tweet out that you'll retweet someone. That's just asking for accolades. Just do it. DM people with tips. Share someone's blog post that tickled your intellect and aroused your joy. Be their hero. Even just for 30 seconds.

SHARE YOUTUBE VIDEOS

✻ ✻ ✻

One of my favorite features of YouTube is the ability to share a video at an exact timestamp. This is a form of social hospitality. Quoting the person (or yourself) and the exact timestamp makes it easy for your followers to click on it and watch it from that exact moment.

Bridget Willard
@BridgetMWillard

"People aren't going to your Instagram bio, your Facebook page, your Twitter profile, if they already know you." Me on @WPwatercooler.

youtu.be/HlWh4B1AW9E?t=...

#Marketing
#BizDev

EP178 - Using Twitter for Lead Gen for WordPress Business...
What's the business application for using Twitter? Can you really grow your business by tweeting? What about Lead ...
youtube.com

9:31 AM · Jan 3, 2021 · Twitter Web App

View Tweet activity

Bridget Willard
@BridgetMWillard

"Open up your home feed and have an intention in your mind." Me with @jasontucker on @WPwatercooler

youtu.be/HlWh4B1AW9E?t=...

#Intent
#Marketing

EP178 - Using Twitter for Lead Gen for WordPress Business...
What's the business application for using Twitter? Can you really grow your business by tweeting? What about Lead ...
youtube.com

4:14 PM · Jan 3, 2021 · Twitter Web App

View Tweet activity

If you've included your Universal Analytics code on your YouTube account, those views will show in Google Analytics, which is really nice.

But you can share videos from other people, too. We love video. But why should we watch this video? When we see tweets with a quote and then a link, we're more inclined to click on it.

Including YouTube in your Twitter Marketing strategy is just smart. Some people don't like to read articles and others never watch video. Have something for everyone, and you'll be the best host ever!

Yes, social media is hospitality.

USE TWITTER FOR BUSINESS DEVELOPMENT

❋ ❋ ❋

If you're not using Twitter Marketing strategies for business development[14], boy you are missing out! It is a gold mine of people who are interested and searching. People are tweeting questions all day long.

Set some time aside once a week to search for questions that you can answer. Then find the latest tweets that look like a good opportunity to reply. Maybe you don't have the best answer but you cc (carbon copy) others and bring them into the conversation.

Bridget Willard
@BridgetMWillard

Replying to @TheJackForge

Yes.

React because Facebook and WordPress.
Angular because "it's better."
VUE because it's fast.

cc @royboy789 **and** @Josh412

1:52 PM · Jan 3, 2021 · Twitter Web App

View Tweet activity

8 Likes

People on Twitter have the intent to learn. Providing helpful information will create that spark of interest that can lead to a bigger conversation.

Listening on Twitter is the best way to validate and update your marketing personas. In all likelihood, your Biz Dev efforts will bring this to the surface.

> "Marketing personas are legitimized stereotypes. When's the last time you updated your company's personas? Instead of relying solely on a marketing persona based upon "Bob," you can actually see what Bob is tweeting about. Bob from 10 years ago liked IPAs; now he collects wine. Time to update the "Bob" persona." Bridget Willard (Willard)

GIVE PEOPLE CREDIT

❋ ❋ ❋

Part of being a polite human being in your Twitter Marketing is giving people credit. That is to say, if you found a very useful article because Robert Nissenbaum tweeted it, then give him credit. On Twitter this is a hat tip or h/t.

THE DEFINITIVE GUIDE TO TWITTER MARKETING

Bridget Willard
@BridgetMWillard

"Gather information, ask for input, and make a decision."
@RandyLyleClark

h/t @rnissenbaum

bit.ly/2COfHUM

#Productivity

Bridget Willard
@BridgetMWillard

@jasontucker You have to read #WPReviewsInRealLife
h/t @LearnWithMattC

Exhibit A:

> **Postmatic** @GoPostmatic · May 19, 2016
> Dinner at friends' house was great and the portions generous. The service was slow, though and no dessert. 1 star. #wpreviewsinreallife

10:45 PM · May 20, 2016 · Twitter Web Client

ıl View Tweet activity

1 Retweet   **3** Likes

 **Bridget Willard**
@BridgetMWillard

The makers of Jif peanut butter team up with Giphy to try to settle the GIF/Jif debate once and for all. via @Verge

bit.ly/32qi648

h/t @sarahpressler

#GIF

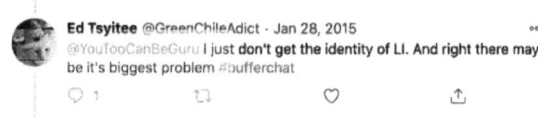 **Ed Tsyitee** @GreenChileAdict · Jan 28, 2015
@YouTooCanBeGuru I just **don't get the identity of LI. And right there may be it's biggest problem** #bufferchat

 **Bridget Willard**
@BridgetMWillard

Replying to @GreenChileAdict

@GreenChileAdict **I used to think of LI as an organic resume. Now I see it as your business card** (h/t @PamAnnMarketing). #BufferChat

11:24 AM · Jan 28, 2015 · Twitter Web Client

Bridget Willard
@BridgetMWillard

Yep h/t @bamadesigner

MT @LeanInOrg: Women are more prone to self-doubt than men ... #LeanIn

> Men apply for jobs when they meet 60% of the hiring criteria, while women wait until they meet 100%.
>
> **LEAN IN**

5:50 PM · Dec 19, 2016 · Twitter Web Client

It's so annoying when you share something and people don't even acknowledge that you were the one who shared it. It's a good way to get unfollowed.

Yes. That's the end of the section. Go and think about this. I'll wait.

USE THE NATIVE APP

❋ ❋ ❋

I love Hootsuite for Twitter Marketing so much. Firstly, because it's free for up to three accounts. Now, I only use it for Twitter because of the column and search features. They allow me to track hashtags, use my lists, and have a search for people tweeting out my website. This is super important if you want to listen to what your customers may be saying or what is resonating. They may have typed your handle wrong or something. You know? Another great thing about Hootsuite is that its mobile app is very similar to the web app.

With that as my only caveat, to be as agile as possible with your Twitter Marketing strategy, it's important to use the native app or web app/page. When Fleets came out (Twitter's version of stories) a lot of people were confused. Why? It was only available on Twitter's mobile app. Any other app didn't show Fleets. It wasn't an option on desktop and certainly wasn't shown in TweetDeck or Hootsuite.

Small UI changes matter. UI changes can affect your metrics and cause you to shift tactics. Hootsuite, for example, doesn't show Twitter Retweet Button retweets. It's so lame. And frustrating to a social media manager. But, Hootsuite is limited by Twitter's API. So, go where the rules are made. It's Twitter's playground.

The one thing you can expect with online marketing is change. Change comes. It comes at the most inconvenient times and the user interface can change dramatically. I mean, remember when Instagram moved the heart (notifications) to the top and swapped that with the shopping bag? We were all pressing the shopping bag for weeks. Muscle memory and UI matters when you're creating a marketing strategy.

> "Twitter management isn't for the faint of heart. It's important to be a practitioner; stay in Twitter as much as possible. This allows you to see any UI/UX and feature changes that Twitter implements. That affects your tactics." Bridget Willard (Willard)

As professionals who market on platforms we cannot control, it is even more important that we use the native platforms as much as possible. In a world full of lazy marketers, being first matters. (Yeah, I said it.)

BE CONSISTENT

❃ ❃ ❃

For Twitter Marketing to be effective, you need to be consistent. This is why I recommend spending time on Twitter every day. Plenty of people follow trends and jump on this bandwagon or that new tech. That's fine. Let people jump over to Hey.com or Parler. The rest of us will stay on Twitter and keep winning for ourselves and our clients.

Consistency is the key in marketing. It's the key in athletics. It's the key in weight loss. It's the key in language learning. Consistency is marketing gold.

People are distracted. You can be the reliable lighthouse they turn to. With that said, it's better to go dark if you're going on vacation and don't plan to respond. Scheduling tweets just to schedule tweets is lame. Be present. Social media managers often help one another out for covering vacation times.

Now, a word about automation. I know, I talk about automation a lot.

In 2011, one of our Twitter friends passed away. He was a big deal. It was the first time I cried and cried over someone I had never met in person. He was consistent. Reliable.

Imad Naffa
@imadnaffa

Imad unexpectedly passed away on Sept 6, 2011, of a heart attack. He was 49 years old. This is @LorettaN, his wife. (In case u didn't know.)

4:25 PM · Dec 5, 2011 · Twitter Web Client

5 Retweets **6** Likes

Though he used automation, he always replied. Unfortunately, because he used automation to tweet out articles with certain keywords, his account kept tweeting after his death. It was very frustrating for his wife.

I schedule out tweets for my clients but only two weeks out. Things happen. Tragedies happen. National emergencies. School shootings. You need to be able to quickly pause your scheduling at any given moment.

FOLLOW PEOPLE IN YOUR INDUSTRY

❋ ❋ ❋

Following others in your industry is an important way to be seen. Twitter is a perfect way to connect with others in your industry. You can find them through search, other people's lists, and/or industry hashtags.

An easy way to find the big names in your industry is to look for event hashtags. (Remember when we had in-person events before COVID?) Those events will list speakers, attendees, and volunteers. People who attend conferences tend to be the industry's movers and shakers. There could be an argument that there are people at home with plenty of expertise, but if they're not tweeting, we'll never really know them. Will we?

Find the hashtag, look at the people using it, follow them, and put them on your list. Follow and list. Follow and list. Pretty soon this behavior will be natural to you. And then people will turn to you for when they're looking for someone to teach their class on Angular or lead the kayaking expedition in the Pacific Northwest.

FOLLOW PEOPLE IN YOUR CITY

❊ ❊ ❊

Following people in your city and creating a list is a great way to understand the local culture. This can be a county or a metropolitan area. When I lived in California, my city only had a population of 28,000. So I also followed people in Orange County and put them on that list.

Spending time on your Twitter list for your city allows you to interact with your local community. You may be invited to speak or meet others who would be great businesses to know. We do business with people we know, like, and trust. This is an aspect of human behavior that is timeless. It won't change when the next big thing comes along.

Even on TikTok, the Texas people follow the Texas people. We like to be around people who choose to live near us.

Following people in your geographic location is even more important if you intend on marketing your business services or products to them. Or if you move like I did. You'll want to assimilate and use the language they do. In California, I would say "Guys!" In Texas, we say "Y'all!" You'll learn about the nuances and about what matters here.

In Texas breakfast tacos are made with bacon. Sausage at the last resort is fine. But they're made with bacon and you get them at the gas station. This isn't like gas station sushi either. It's legit. No joke. Laredo Taco is inside Stripes (the gas station). You'll want to learn about your new culture before you start making a faux pas.

SPEND 5 MINUTES A DAY IN YOUR HOME FEED

❋ ❋ ❋

Twitter Marketing is a lifestyle, not a quick fix. You'll want to work it into your daily schedule. I always recommend people spend five minutes in the morning and five after lunch. It really depends on how fast you want to grow. Twitter is a numbers and volume game. If you're not treating Twitter seriously, you probably don't have any notifications anyway. Oh yeah, when you get serious, don't get push notifications. That will drive you crazy.

One of the good things about spending time in your home feed is that you see opportunities. I started to notice, for example, that people were really struggling with writing their own speaker bios. This was during the heavy conference season for WordCamps, so I offered to write their bio for them.

This gave birth to six bios so I tweeted again. So then I expanded my secret menu. I mean, if In-N-Out can have one, why can't I? I began writing page content, editing WordCamp talk pitches, and more! That cash always came in handy. Especially during the building of my business and inevitable client loss.

>
> **Bridget Willard**
> @BridgetMWillard
>
> My Secret Menu (Fast, **Fast PayPal Cash**)
>
> * Write Speaker Bios $25
> * Edit WordCamp Pitches **$40**
> * Write Page Content $50
> * Short-form blog posts **(300-500)** $100
>
> #Marketing
> #WordPress
> #SmallBiz
>
> 12:35 AM · May 20, 2019 · Minideck
>
> View Tweet activity
>
> **4** Retweets   **1** Quote Tweet   **10** Likes

By now, I've written over 40 speaker bios for many of the people in WordPress you'd recognize. Because of that, I was asked to give a workshop at WordCamp US to teach people how to write[15] a friendly bio of themselves.

Even if your intention on spending time in the home feed isn't business development, you'll pass by people in the halls of the Internet you never would have noticed otherwise. This world is a lovely, full place. There are so many amazing people to get to know.

LOG IN WITH INTENT

* * *

When you begin anything intent drives the results. This is because we do what we practice. If your intent is to become a better writer, then text your friends in complete sentences. If your intent is to practice mindfulness, then set an alarm for meditation. If your intent is to hit a home run, then look at where you want the ball to end up. Intent matters.

Twitter marketing without intent is aimless and purposeless. You'll feel drained and bored. You'll get sucked into mini debates about politics or how to pronounce "GIF." Chunks of time will pass by without any real results. You haven't helped your brand. You haven't given back to the world. You haven't encouraged someone.

Level up your Twitter Marketing by logging in with the intent to be helpful. Find two or three tweets that you can reply to every day. Yes, every day. Twitter works if you work it.[16]

LOOK AT YOUR ANALYTICS

❃ ❃ ❃

Data is important but it needs context. Google analytics or Twitter analytics -- neither are the be-all, end-all. However, you'll want to look at your data sets and compare and contrast them.

The caveat to data is that data only comes from what is measured. Some people browse in private mode. They search the Internet on duckduckgo.com or yahoo.com instead of Google. They don't use Gmail. They may take out their SIM cards all the time or swap them out. Maybe they turn off their WiFi at night or have masking routers.

Data is a picture of the past. This is why spending time online interacting with your audience is so important. This is how you get data in real-time. This is data as it happens. People grow and evolve. Data is an autopsy. What are people doing now?

Another problem with data is that it only shows what you've done. If you have only tweeted on Tuesdays, then Tuesday is your best day. Beyond what you measure, and what will inevitably be excluded, you can't measure affinity. You can't measure brand awareness. You don't know what people are thinking.

What I do like is the tweets to profile visit ratio. This tells me that people have seen a tweet and gone to the profile.

> "I like the tweets to profile visit ratio to be above .20. The profile visits [metric] is important because it means that a user saw your tweet, clicked on your username/handle, and then looked at your profile." Bridget Willard

CYCLE YOUR CONTENT

✽ ✽ ✽

The best way to cycle your content is to share it with different copy and hashtags. It may hit someone at a different phase in their life or business cycle.

The most important part of Twitter Marketing is staying top of mind. Meaning, you want them to see your tweet when they're trying to remember who bakes those crazy cakes. Wait, I forgot to ask her about copywriting. Oh yeah, I was thinking about buying lockers. Oh cool, I'll refer my client to that person for their website build.

 **Bridget** Willard
@BridgetMWillard

Time and time again, I am asked how to be more efficient in one's use of Twitter. The answer is simple. Use lists.

bridgetwillard.com/twitterlists/

#Twitter

Be More Efficient on Twitter with Twitter Lists - Bridget Willard
Twitter lists are the most efficient way to use Twitter for the busy marketing

Bridget Willard
@BridgetMWillard

If you only read one blog post of mine, read this.

bridgetwillard.com/twitterlists/

#SmallBiz
#Marketing

Be More Efficient on Twitter with Twitter Lists - Bridget Willard
Twitter lists are the most efficient way to use Twitter for the busy marketing

Resist the temptation to retweet yourself. First of all, it looks really self-centered. Also, if it didn't hit your audience the first time, maybe rewrite the tweet. This seems obvious but I've been in some very, um, tense conversations on Twitter about this. I mean, do you, Boo. But then again you're reading my tips. So. What's the worst-case scenario? Try it my way for a month and if you don't like it, I'll give you your money back. Also, did you know that any user can turn your retweets off? It's true.

When it comes to cycling your content and a plugin like Revive Old Posts[17], be sure to make the time interval an odd number. If you start sharing tweets at 8:00 AM and set it up with an eight-hour interval, then your tweets will go out every eight hours. Meaning, your blog post will be put out on Twitter at 8:00 AM, 4:00 PM, and midnight every single day. That limits who has an opportunity to see your tweets.

I always use an odd number with a half for my interval settings on Revive Old Posts. I am always changing my frequency between 7.5 hours, 13.5 hours, 17.5 hours, and 23.5 hours. Sometimes, I just want to test the waters or adjust for the volume of tweets I'm adding in real-time. Test it out for yourself.

DON'T USE THE RETWEET BUTTON

✤ ✤ ✤

Twitter existed before the Retweet Button. I have a whole blog post that goes into great depth on why you shouldn't use the Retweet Button.[18] It's even a featured snippet on Google. (Yep. I'm pretty proud of that.

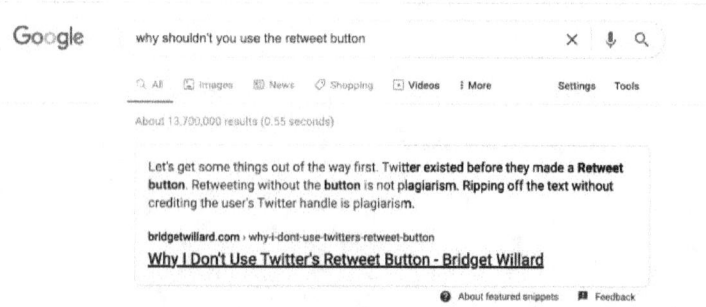

Your Twitter Marketing is stunted with the Retweet

Button (not the comment retweet, but a plain retweet). Here's why. The retweet button ends a conversation. There is no way to reply. You get a notification that someone retweeted you. But you can't reply. At least, you can't easily reply.

To reply to a retweet, you have to click on the person, start a tweet, and then thank them. I used to do it all of the time. Sometimes I still do. It's so much better to make your own tweet. You want people to see your face in their Twitter feed. You want your logo to be recognized in the Twitter feed. That's Branding 101. So, why would you share someone else's flyer at your event?

BE PATIENT

❖ ❖ ❖

Seriously. Trying Twitter for one month isn't long enough, my friend. It is a big part of your whole marketing. You probably won't see a rise in clicks until about month three. Business comes later. This is for the longevity of your business. Not just for today.

"Stop looking for tangible results." Bridget Willard (Resnick)

There is no such thing as a first-click lead. No one is going to see your tweet for the first time, click on it, see your thing, and buy it immediately. It takes 7-10 touches to make a sale at the very minimum. It always has and it always will. Why? Because the humans behind the screen are still, well, human.

"You'll never get first-click leads from Twitter. I say never, but it's probably an exaggeration. Asking social media to solve your lead-generation problem is short-sighted at best. First of all, it will fail — miserably. Secondly, your focus on leads will cause you to consciously or even subconsciously make decisions out of fear and desperation. Those are almost never good decisions." Bridget Willard (Willard)

TWITTER MARKETING IS A LONG GAME!

❋ ❋ ❋

Twitter brings a brand awareness component that raises the effectiveness of all of your marketing efforts.

Our marketing efforts are only a failure when we quit.

BIBLIOGRAPHY

Resnick, Jason. "S03 E09 - Bridget Willard on WordPress, Why Twitter is the Best, and Relationship Marketing." *Rezzz.com*, https://rezzz.com/podcast/bridget-willard-on-wordpress-why-twitter-is-the-best-and-relationship-marketing. Accessed 4 Jan 2021.

Stephen, Carol. "Baby Boomers and Social Media." *YourSocialMedia.com*, 31 Oct 2013, https://yoursocialmediaworks.com/baby-boomers-and-social-media.

Stephen, Carol. "A Short History of the #DigiBlogChat Twitter Chat." *YourSocialMediaWorks.com*, 17 Dec 2020, https://yoursocialmediaworks.com/a-short-history-of-the-digiblogchat-twitter-chat.

TED.com, and Simon Sinek. "Why Good Leaders Make You Feel Safe." *TED.com*, 1 Mar 2014, https://www.ted.com/talks/simon_sinek_why_good_leaders_make_you_feel_safe.

Willard, Bridget. "5 Reasons to use Twitter Animated GIFs for Your Brand." *BridgetWillard.com*, 15 May 2020, https://bridgetwillard.com/twitter-animated-gifs-brand/.

Willard, Bridget. "Leadership Through Following – A Twitter Strategy." *BridgetWillard.com*, 25 May 2014, https://bridgetwillard.com/leadership-through-following-a-twitter-strategy/.

Willard, Bridget. "Leads from Social: Affinity, Discovery, and Validation." *BridgetWillard.com*, 20 May 2017, https://bridgetwillard.com/leads-social-affinity-discovery-validation/.

Willard, Bridget. "Protect Your Brand. It's Not a Joke." *BridgetWillard.com*, 3 Jan 2018, https://bridgetwillard.com/protect-your-brand-its-not-a-joke/.

Willard, Bridget. "Twitter is the Best Platform for B2B Marketing." *BridgetWillard.com*, 8 Nov 2017, https://bridgetwillard.com/twitter-b2b-marketing-five-reasons/.

Willard, Bridget. "Twitter Management Tools – Here Are My 11 Tools." *BridgetWillard.com*, 19 Jun 2020, https://bridgetwillard.com/twitter-management-tools/.

Willard, Bridget. "What Makes a Twitter Profile Good?" *BridgetWillard.com*, 11 May 2016, https://bridgetwillard.com/makes-twitter-profile-good/.

Willard, Bridget. "Why I Don't Use Twitter's Retweet Button." *BridgetWillard.com*, 18 Mar 2013, https://bridgetwillard.com/why-i-dont-use-twitters-retweet-button/.

WPwatercooler Network. "EP178 – Using Twitter for Lead Gen for WordPress Businesses." *WPwatercooler.com*, 4 Dec 2020, https://www.wpwatercooler.com/smartmarketingshow/ep178-using-twitter-for-lead-gen-for-wordpress-businesses/.

"Your Business Marketing Should Include Twitter." *BridgetWillard.com*, 30 May 2019, https://bridgetwillard.com/your-business-marketing-should-include-twitter/.

---

[1] https://twitter.com/BridgetMWillard
[2] https://bit.ly/LearnTwitter2020
[3] https://en.wikipedia.org/wiki/Dian_Fossey
[4] https://twitter.com/rigginsconst
[5] https://bridgetwillard.com/twitterlists/
[6] https://youtu.be/sadYkEqdC98
[7] https://bridgetwillard.com/correctly-format-blog-post/
[8] https://wordpress.org/plugins/tweet-old-post/
[9] https://ga-dev-tools.appspot.com/campaign-url-builder/
[10] https://twitter.com/search?q=%23DigiBlogChat&src=hashtag_click
[11] https://yoursocialmediaworks.com/a-short-history-of-the-digiblogchat-twitter-chat
[12] https://twitter.com/search?q=%23ConstChat&src=typed_query
[13] https://bridgetwillard.com/best-seo-advice-nonprofits-np-chat/
[14] https://youtu.be/9KdnEdtGvKg
[15] https://wordpress.tv/2019/11/19/bridget-willard-crafting-an-effective-bio-for-your-website-and-social-profiles-part-1/
[16] https://bridgetwillard.com/yep-twitter-works-if-you-work-it/
[17] https://wordpress.org/plugins/tweet-old-post/
[18] https://bridgetwillard.com/why-i-dont-use-twitters-retweet-button/

ABOUT THE AUTHOR

Bridget Willard

Bridget Willard is a marketing consultant who brings her vast background together to help small businesses. She has worked in construction, franchise development, nonprofits, and tech. She is especially known for her brand building for  Riggins Construction, GiveWP, and the Make WordPress Marketing Team.

Bridget co-hosts The Smart Marketing Show with Jason Tucker -- a podcast on the WPwatercooler network.

When she's not writing about marketing, she is spending time with her friends, changing her hair style, learning languages on Duolingo, or walking in nature.

Say hi to her on Twitter at @BridgetMWillard and check out her site at bridgetwillard.com.

www.ingramcontent.com/pod-product-compliance
Lightning Source LLC
Chambersburg PA
CBHW070434220526
45466CB00004B/1666